KIDS LOVE MUSIC CRAFTS

Joanna Ponto and Felicia Lowenstein Niven

Enslow Publishing
101 W. 23rd Street
Suite 240
New York, NY 10011
USA

enslow.com

Published in 2019 by Enslow Publishing, LLC.
101 W. 23rd Street, Suite 240, New York, NY 10011

Library of Congress Cataloging-in-Publication Data

Names: Ponto, Joanna, author. | Niven, Felicia Lowenstein, author.
Title: Kids love music crafts / Joanna Ponto and Felicia Lowenstein Niven.
Description: New York : Enslow Publishing, 2019. | Series: Kids love crafts
  | Audience: Grades 3-5.
Includes bibliographical references and index.
Identifiers: LCCN 2018014691| ISBN 9781978501997 (library bound) |
  ISBN 9781978502833 (pbk.) | ISBN 9781978502840 (6 pack)
Subjects: LCSH: Musical instruments–Construction–Juvenile literature.
Classification: LCC ML460 .P82 2019 | DDC 372.87–dc23
LC record available at https://lccn.loc.gov/2018014691

Printed in the United States of America

To Our Readers: We have done our best to make sure all website addresses in this book were active and appropriate when we went to press. However, the author and the publisher have no control over and assume no liability for the material available on those websites or on any websites they may link to. Any comments or suggestions can be sent by email to customerservice@enslow.com.

Portions of this book appeared in *Nifty Thrifty Music Crafts*.

Photo Credits: Crafts on cover and throughout book prepared by June Ponte; photography by Nicole DiMella/Enslow Publishing, LLC; p. 5 Loza-koza/Shutterstock.com; design elements on cover and throughout book: Betelgejze/Shutterstock.com (series logo), Chinch/Shutterstock.com (torn rainbow paper border), daisybee/Shutterstock.com (colorful letters), Iuliia Aseeva/Shutterstock.com ("love" in series and book titles), Yulia M./Shutterstock.com (colorful numbers).

Safety Note:

Be sure to **ask for help from an adult**, if needed, to complete these crafts!

CONTENTS

MAKING MUSIC!

It is impossible to know exactly by whom or when music was invented. The earliest musical instruments, bone flutes, are about forty thousand to sixty thousand years old, but music itself is much older. Humans probably made music by singing, clapping, or hitting their hands on different things around them to communicate before they invented language.

But people aren't the only species to make music! You've probably heard the lovely melodies made by songbirds such as the canary, finch, and robin. Humpback whales produce long, loud notes that can travel 100 miles (161 kilometers) across the ocean. Crickets chirp by rubbing their wings together. Monkeys called macaques drum by shaking branches or banging on logs to let other monkeys know they're in charge.

There are many different kinds of instruments throughout the world, but they are put into three main groups: percussion, string, and wind. Percussion instruments, such as a drum, are struck, shaken, or rubbed. String instruments are either plucked or played with a bow, such as violins and guitars. These produce sound when their strings vibrate. Wind instruments produce sound when air is blown into them, as in the trumpet, or across them, as in the flute.

The flute is a popular wind instrument children learn to play in school bands.

Genres, or types, of music include classical, jazz, rhythm and blues, rock and roll, pop, hip-hop, heavy metal, country, reggae, electronic, and many others. You may listen to certain music that matches your mood. Or maybe you put something on that changes your mood, like when you're sad and you listen to a lively, upbeat song to put a smile on your face.

Each craft in this book is a working instrument. Learn fascinating facts about the origin of each instrument as you create them. You can make beautiful music to share with family and friends!

GLASS JAR XYLOPHONE

A xylophone is a percussion instrument made up of wooden, bamboo, or metal bars of different lengths. When hit with a mallet, each bar produces a different sound. Many experts believe that the first xylophones originated in Asia in the ninth century and then spread to Africa. This project uses glass jars filled with different amounts of water to produce different sounds. **Tap the jars gently so you don't break them.**

WHAT YOU WILL NEED:

- long piece of felt or cloth
- 6 empty glass jars, any size
- puff paint (optional)
- ribbon (optional)
- water
- food coloring (optional)
- unsharpened pencil, craft stick, or chopstick
- metal spoon

WHAT TO DO:

1 On the felt, arrange the jars in one long line so there is about 2 inches (5 centimeters) in between each jar (see **A**). If you wish, tie ribbon around each jar and decorate (see **B**).

A

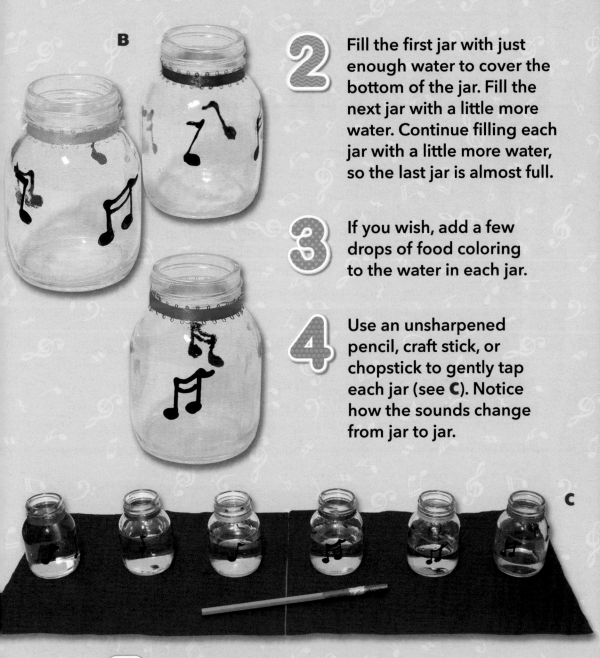

B

2 Fill the first jar with just enough water to cover the bottom of the jar. Fill the next jar with a little more water. Continue filling each jar with a little more water, so the last jar is almost full.

3 If you wish, add a few drops of food coloring to the water in each jar.

4 Use an unsharpened pencil, craft stick, or chopstick to gently tap each jar (see **C**). Notice how the sounds change from jar to jar.

C

5 Next, try the metal spoon. Tap the jars gently. What sounds can you make?

SANDPAPER RHYTHM BLOCKS

Sandpaper rhythm blocks are two wooden blocks covered in sandpaper that are rubbed together to produce sound. The roughness of the sandpaper affects the volume: the rougher the sandpaper, the louder the sound. Rhythm blocks are percussion instruments and originated in the United States in the early twentieth century. They were used to make sound effects for stage performances before musicians adopted them as instruments. Make your own pair of rhythm blocks to play to the beat!

WHAT YOU WILL NEED:

- marker
- 2 small cereal boxes
- sandpaper
- scissors
- tacky craft glue
- poster paint (optional)
- paintbrush (optional)

WHAT TO DO:

1 With the marker, trace the shape of each small cereal box on the sandpaper (see **A**). (See page 28 for the pattern.) Cut out both shapes.

A

8

2 Ask an adult for help. Apply tacky craft glue to one side of each box.

3 Place the sandpaper, smooth side down, onto the box. Do the same with the other piece of sandpaper. Trim the sandpaper edges if needed (see **B**). Let dry.

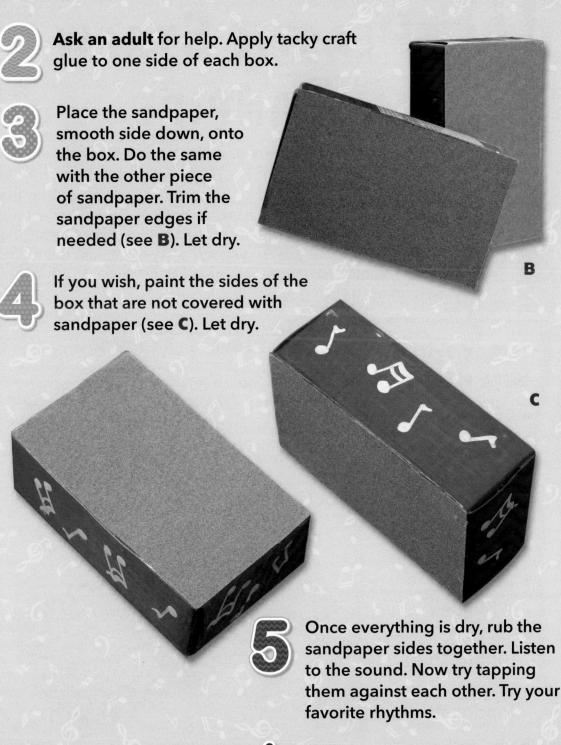

B

4 If you wish, paint the sides of the box that are not covered with sandpaper (see **C**). Let dry.

C

5 Once everything is dry, rub the sandpaper sides together. Listen to the sound. Now try tapping them against each other. Try your favorite rhythms.

PLASTIC STRAW PANPIPE

The panpipe, also called a syrinx or pan flute, is a wind instrument made up of pipes of different lengths tied together in a row. It was first used by ancient Greek shepherds in the third millennium BCE. It is named after Pan, the god of nature, who is said to have invented it. The bottoms of the pipes are usually sealed with wax, so you have to blow across the top to make a sound. Because each pipe is a different length, the pitch will change as you go from side to side.

WHAT YOU WILL NEED:

- 10 drinking straws
- masking tape
- scissors
- modeling clay or play dough
- feathers (optional)
- stickers (optional)
- ribbon (optional)

WHAT TO DO:

1 Line up ten drinking straws. Tape the straws together about an inch (2½ cm) from the top using masking tape (see **A**).

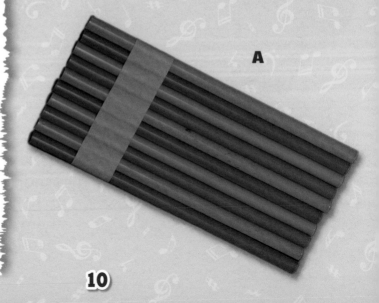

A

B

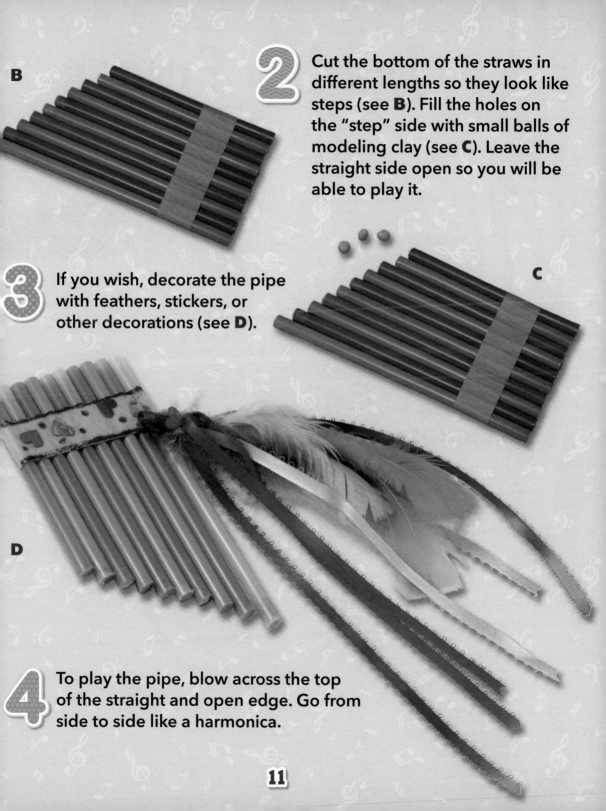

2 Cut the bottom of the straws in different lengths so they look like steps (see **B**). Fill the holes on the "step" side with small balls of modeling clay (see **C**). Leave the straight side open so you will be able to play it.

3 If you wish, decorate the pipe with feathers, stickers, or other decorations (see **D**).

C

D

4 To play the pipe, blow across the top of the straight and open edge. Go from side to side like a harmonica.

JAR LID FINGER CYMBALS

Finger cymbals, also called *zills*, are small metal disks worn on the thumb and middle finger of each hand. They are percussion instruments. Belly dancers strike them together in a pattern as they dance. When people hear finger cymbals, they usually think of Middle Eastern music. But Tibetan Buddhists also use them, called *tingsha*, in prayer and rituals. Try these simple jar lid finger cymbals and add a little something extra special to your music.

WHAT YOU WILL NEED:

- elastic
- ruler
- scissors
- 2 metal jar lids or bottle caps, washed and dried
- white glue
- masking tape
- puff paint (optional)

WHAT TO DO:

 Measure and cut two pieces of elastic about 3 inches (8 cm) long.

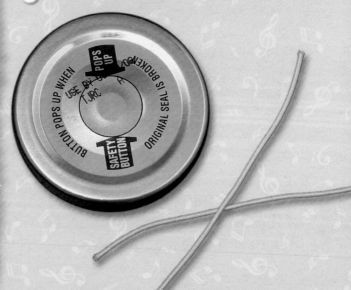

Make a loop with one piece of elastic and glue the ends to the inside of the metal jar lid. Do the same with the other piece of elastic and other lid. Let dry. Use a small piece of masking tape to make sure the elastic stays in place. If you wish, decorate the lids.

Put one cymbal on your thumb. Put the other cymbal on your middle finger of the same hand. You are ready to follow a beat!

COFFEE CAN COLONIAL DRUM

Drummers were an important part of the colonial army. Since there were no radios back then, soldiers used music to communicate with each other over long distances. Drummers of the American Revolutionary War (1775-1783) were usually boys between ten and eighteen years old. Soldiers marched to the beat of the drum, keeping them together. Besides helping troops during training exercises, colonial drummers also sounded signals, alarms, and times of day. On the battlefield, the beat of the drum told soldiers to turn left or right, fire their guns, stop firing, or let the enemy know they wanted to surrender. Keep the beat with this colorful coffee can colonial drum.

WHAT YOU WILL NEED:

- balloon
- scissors
- coffee or soup can, washed and dried
- duct tape
- construction paper (optional)
- white glue (optional)
- glitter (optional)
- markers (optional)
- rope or yarn
- 2 unsharpened pencils, chopsticks, or straws

WHAT TO DO:

1 **Ask an adult** to blow up the balloon. Let the air out. This will help stretch it. Cut straight across the balloon, cutting off the bottom (see **A**). Stretch the balloon tightly across the open part of the coffee or soup can so it covers the opening. Use duct tape to tape the edges down (see **B**). **Ask an adult** to help you so the balloon stays tight.

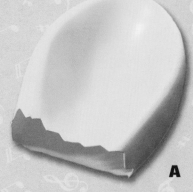

A

2 If you wish, carefully decorate the can. Glue construction paper around the can. Let dry. Use glitter or markers to decorate the paper. Let dry.

B

C

3 Measure a piece of rope or yarn by loosely wrapping it twice around your waist. Place the middle of the rope around the can and tie a knot (see **C**). Use the ends of the rope to make a bow around your waist.

4 Try a few rhythms with the pencils, chopsticks, or straws. You are ready to march!

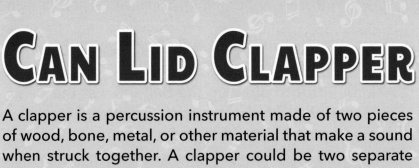

CAN LID CLAPPER

A clapper is a percussion instrument made of two pieces of wood, bone, metal, or other material that make a sound when struck together. A clapper could be two separate pieces held in each hand or two pieces tied together and held in one hand. They have been around for thousands of years and have been used by many cultures around the world. Ancient Egyptians had some made from ivory and shaped like arms and hands. Hawaiians clicked two small stones together. Native Americans split a branch partway down the center and hit it against their hands. Make your own one-handed clapper.

WHAT YOU WILL NEED:

- pencil
- 2 lids from a frozen juice can
- cardboard from a cereal box
- scissors
- white glue
- masking tape
- 2 craft sticks
- markers (optional)

WHAT TO DO:

1 With a pencil, trace the shape of each lid on the cardboard (see page 26 for the pattern). Cut out the two circles (see **A**).

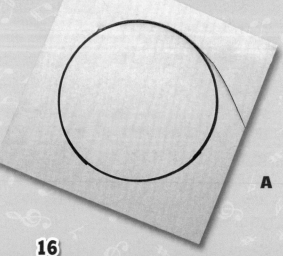

A

16

B

2 Glue or tape one circle to one lid (see **B**). Do the same with the other circle and lid. Let dry.

3 Glue or tape one craft stick to the cardboard side of each lid. Let dry.

4 Position the sticks so the lids face each other. Tape the bottom of the craft sticks together (see **C**).

C

5 If you wish, decorate the cardboard side and craft sticks of the clapper using markers or other decorations (see **D**). Let dry.

D

6 Shake the clapper or hit it against your hand to make a sound.

PIE PLATE TAMBOURINE

A tambourine kind of looks like a drum, but it has jingles. This percussion instrument was invented in the Middle East thousands of years ago. In ancient Egypt, temple dancers played them in religious ceremonies. Other early civilizations used the tambourine in festivals and funerals. During the Middle Ages, tambourines were often played by traveling performers. Today, tambourines are used in gospel, pop, and rock and roll. Play your homemade tambourine by shaking it or hitting it against your palm or leg.

WHAT YOU WILL NEED:

- marker
- 1 disposable aluminum pie plate
- ruler
- hole punch
- 5 pipe cleaners or 10 twist ties
- scissors
- 20 1-inch (2½ cm) metal washers or 10 medium-sized jingle bells
- ribbon (optional)

WHAT TO DO:

1 With the marker, make sixteen evenly spaced dots around the edge of a pie plate. Use the hole punch to punch out the holes. **Ask an adult** for help.

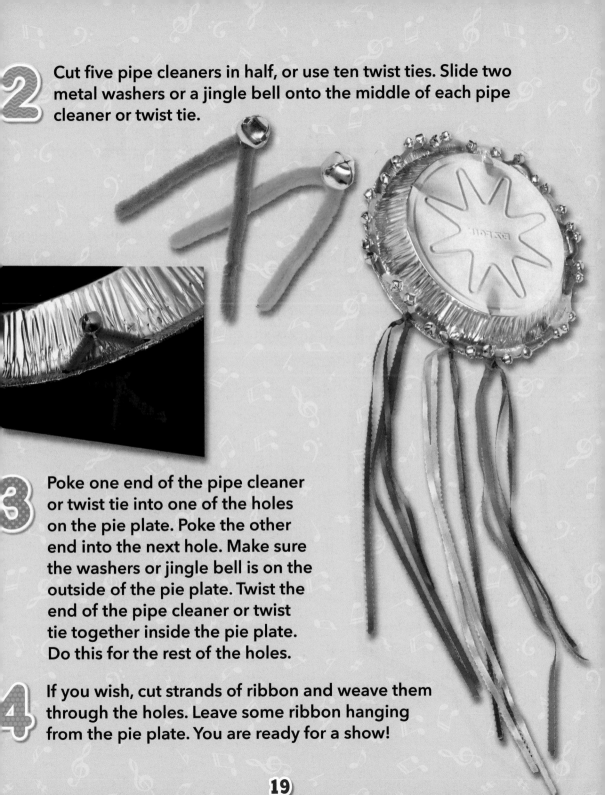

2 Cut five pipe cleaners in half, or use ten twist ties. Slide two metal washers or a jingle bell onto the middle of each pipe cleaner or twist tie.

3 Poke one end of the pipe cleaner or twist tie into one of the holes on the pie plate. Poke the other end into the next hole. Make sure the washers or jingle bell is on the outside of the pie plate. Twist the end of the pipe cleaner or twist tie together inside the pie plate. Do this for the rest of the holes.

4 If you wish, cut strands of ribbon and weave them through the holes. Leave some ribbon hanging from the pie plate. You are ready for a show!

PAPER TOWEL TUBE RAIN STICK

A rain stick is a percussion instrument made of a hollowed plant stalk, such as cactus or bamboo, filled with pebbles or seeds. When turned or shaken, it produces a sound like falling rain. It is thought that ancient peoples who lived in desert climates used these instruments in rituals to bring rain. They are still used by Native Americans in Mexico, South America, and the southwestern United States. You can make your own rain stick with a paper towel tube and uncooked rice.

WHAT YOU WILL NEED:

- aluminum foil
- paper towel tube
- ruler
- scissors
- clear tape
- 1 cup (185 grams) uncooked rice
- feathers (optional)
- glitter (optional)
- markers (optional)

WHAT TO DO:

1 Squeeze a piece of 12-inch × 12-inch (30½ × 30½ cm) aluminum foil into a long snake-like shape (see pattern on page 27). Coil the foil snake so it looks like a spring (see **A**). Make it narrow enough to fit in the paper towel tube. Put the foil spring into the paper towel tube. It should fill the tube from top to bottom. If it does not, add another coiled foil snake.

A

2 Cut out two 4-inch × 4-inch (10 × 10 cm) squares of foil (see pattern on page 26). Cover one end of the tube with one square of foil (see **B**). Use clear tape to tape the foil in place.

3 Pour in 1 cup of uncooked rice (see **C**).

B

C

4 Cover the open end of the tube with the second square of foil. Use clear tape to tape the foil in place.

5 If you wish, decorate the rain stick using feathers, glitter, and markers (see **D**). Let dry.

D

JUICE CAN MARACAS

Maracas are a pair of percussion instruments that look and sound like rattles. They were invented by the original people of Puerto Rico, the Tainos. They made them out of the dried-out shells of a small fruit called the higuera. The shells were filled with pebbles and attached to a handle. Today, maracas are plastic or wood. The maracas are one of the most important instruments in salsa music and add an exciting rhythm to other kinds of music from the Caribbean and Latin America. Make and shake these amazing maracas!

WHAT YOU WILL NEED:

- 2 empty frozen juice cans with lids, washed and dried
- uncooked corn, rice, or dried beans
- light cardboard
- scissors
- hole punch
- pencil
- 2 unsharpened pencils
- masking tape
- tissue paper, any color
- white glue
- paintbrush
- glue wash (1 part white glue, 1 part water)

WHAT TO DO:

1 Remove one lid from one juice can (see **A**). Fill the can one third of the way with uncooked corn, rice, or dried beans.

A

2 Trace the lid of the juice can onto a piece of cardboard. Cut it out. **Ask an adult** to carefully punch a hole in the center of the circle.

3 Fit the unsharpened pencil through the hole. Place the cardboard with the pencil on the open end of the juice can. Use masking tape to secure the cardboard to the juice can (see **B**).

B

4 Tear tissue paper into different sizes. Put the juice can down with the pencil sticking up. Brush glue onto the juice can and a little bit of the pencil. Place the tissue paper pieces all over the glue. Be sure to overlap the pieces. Let dry. Cover the top of the can with glue and cover with tissue paper (see **C**). Let dry. Brush a glue wash over the entire can. Let dry.

5 Repeat steps 1 to 4 for the second juice can.

6 Give the dry juice cans a gentle shake. You are now ready to play a salsa rhythm!

C

CEREAL BOX UKULELE

The ukulele is a small guitar with four strings often heard Hawaiian music. But it was actually invented in Portugal an originally known as the machete (ma CHET). In the 1800 Portuguese immigrants moved to Hawaii to work its plantatio and factories, and woodworkers started making the instrument which became very popular with the local people. *Ukelele* mear "jumping flea" in Hawaiian, probably because fingers appear fly from string to string when playing it. Recreate the sounds of th tropical islands with this easy ukulele crafted from a cereal box!

WHAT YOU WILL NEED:

- cereal box
- pencil
- scissors
- paper towel tube
- poster paint
- paintbrush
- markers
- 4 long rubber bands (and extras in case they break)
- masking tape

WHAT TO DO:

1 Draw a circle or oval on the cereal box. Carefully cut out the circle or oval (see **Ask an adult** for help.

A

2 Using poster paint, paint the cereal box and paper towel tube. Let dry. Use markers to make designs (see pattern on page 29). Let dry.

3 Stretch four long rubber bands so they fit over the box the long way (see **B**). Pluck a band to see how it sounds.

4 Take the paper towel tube. Carefully, cut two slits along the bottom about 2 inches (5 cm) long. Fold back the sides.

5 Press the sides against one end of the box to make a handle. Tape the sides down using masking tape. Use markers or poster paint to cover the masking tape. Let dry (see **C**).

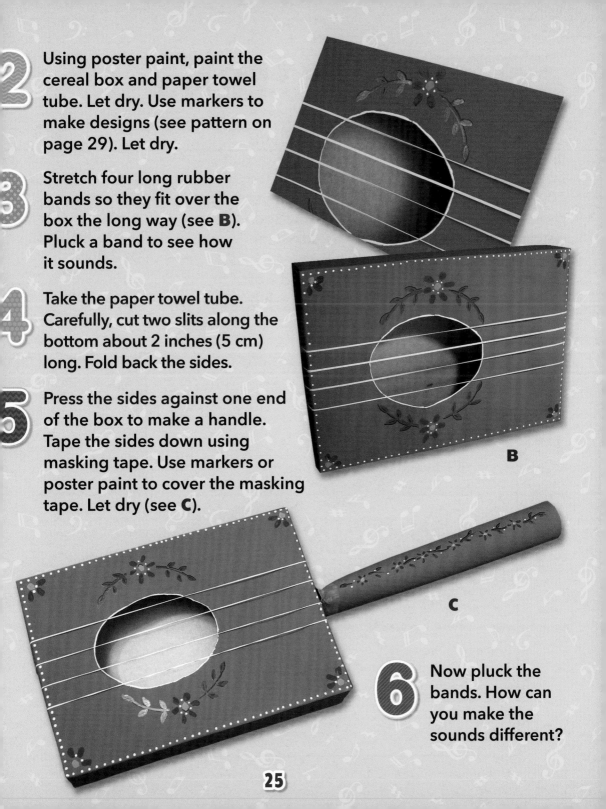

B

C

6 Now pluck the bands. How can you make the sounds different?

PATTERNS

The percentages included on the patterns tell you how much to enlarge or shrink the image using a copier. (The patterns that say 100% are at the correct size as they are.) Most copiers and printers have an adjustable size/percentage feature to change the size of an image when you print it. After you print the patterns to their true sizes, cut them out or use tracing paper to copy them. **Ask an adult** to help you trace and cut the shapes.

**Can Lid Clapper
at 100%**

**Paper Towel Tube Rain Stick
at 100%
(cut from aluminum foil,
4 × 4 inches [10 × 10 cm])**

Paper Towel Tube Rain Stick
enlarge 200%
(cut from aluminum foil,
12 × 12 inches [30½ × 30½ cm])

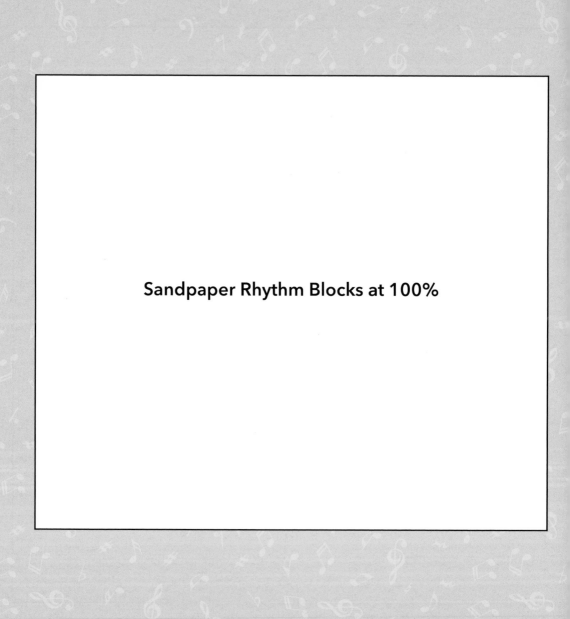

Sandpaper Rhythm Blocks at 100%

Cereal Box Ukulele at 100%

LEARN MORE

BOOKS

Owen, Ruth. *I Can Start a Band!* New York, NY: Windmill Books, 2017.

Rau, Dana Meachen. *Making Musical Instruments.* North Mankato, MN: Cherry Lake Publishing, 2016.

Reid, Emily. *I Can Make Musical Instruments.* New York, NY: Windmill Books, 2015.

Sjonger, Rebecca. *Maker Projects for Kids Who Love Music.* New York, NY: Crabtree Publishing Company, 2016.

WEBSITES

DLTK's Crafts for Kids
www.dltk-kids.com/crafts/music/index.htm
Craft an African drum, bird rattle, and other projects or print out music-themed coloring pages.

Free Kids Crafts
www.freekidscrafts.com/school-days/music-crafts
Learn to make a door harp, cardboard tube kazoo, Australian didgeridoo, and other fun musical instruments.

Kinder Art
kinderart.com/art-lessons/music/
easy-make-musical-instruments
Create an Egyptian sistrum, Chinese gong, and several different kinds of drums and maracas.

INDEX